GOODMAN'S FIVE-STAR STORIES

TRAVELS

8 Stories from Around the World

With TESTS to Help You Read and Write

W9-BRW-328

by Burton Goodman

JAMESTOWN PUBLISHERS

a division of NTC/CONTEMPORARY PUBLISHING GROUP
Lincolnwood, Illinois USA

TITLES IN THE SERIES

Travels	Level A	Shocks	Level E
More Travels	Level A	After Shocks	Level E
Adventures	Level B	Sudden Twists	Level F
More Adventures	Level B	More Twists	Level F
Chills	Level C	Encounters	Level G
More Chills	Level C	More Encounters	Level G
Surprises	Level D	Conflicts	Level H
More Surprises	Level D	More Conflicts	Level H

Cover illustration: David Cunningham
Interior illustrations: Jim Abel, James Buckley, Yoshi Miyake, Jeff Stern

Acknowledgments are on page 124, which is to be considered an extension of this copyright page.

ISBN: 0-89061-644-2

Published by Jamestown Publishers,
a division of NTC/Contemporary Publishing Group, Inc.,
4255 West Touhy Avenue,
Lincolnwood (Chicago), Illinois 60712-1975 U.S.A.
© 1999 by Burton Goodman
All rights reserved. No part of this book may be reproduced,
stored in a retrieval system, or transmitted in any form or by any means,
electronic, mechanical, photocopying, recording, or otherwise,
without prior permission of the publisher.
Manufactured in the United States of America.

5 6 7 8 9 10 11 12 13 14 100 / 055 11 10 9 08 07 06 05

Contents

To the Reader

There are eight stories in this book. They come from around the world. I picked these stories because I like them very much. I think that you will like them too.

The stories are fun to read. The exercises will be fun to do too. They will help you read and write better. You will also find out about the parts of a story such as the *plot*.

First go over the words in **Before You Read**. Make sure you know what each word means. This will help when you read the story.

Later, do the exercises after each of the stories. See how well you do on these TESTS:

TELL ABOUT THE STORY.

END EACH LINE.

SHOW WHAT WORDS MEAN.

THINK ABOUT THE STORY.

SPOT PARTS OF A STORY.

TELL ABOUT THE STORY helps you find things that happened in the story. These are sometimes called *facts*.

END EACH LINE helps you with your reading and vocabulary (what words mean). This part uses fill-in, or cloze, exercises.

SHOW WHAT WORDS MEAN helps you build your vocabulary. The vocabulary words in each story are in **dark letters.** You may look back at these words when you do the vocabulary questions.

THINK ABOUT THE STORY asks *critical thinking* questions. This means you will have to think about what happened in the story. Then you will have to work out the answers.

SPOT PARTS OF A STORY goes over *character, plot,* and *setting.* On page 3 you will find the meanings of these words. You may look back at the meanings when you do the questions.

There is one other part. It is called THINK SOME MORE ABOUT THE STORY. This part helps you to think, talk, and *write* about the story.

There are four questions for each of the TESTS exercises. Here is the way to do the exercises:

- Do all the exercises.

- Go over your answers with your teacher.

- At the end of each exercise, write in your score for that exercise. Each question is worth 5 points. There are four questions, so you can get up to 20 points.

- You will find a TESTS chart after all of the exercises. Use this chart to add up your TOTAL SCORE. If you get all the questions right, your score will be 100.

- Keep track of how well you do. First write your TOTAL SCORE on the **Progress Chart** on page 120. Then write your score on the **Progress Graph** on page 121. Look at the **Progress Graph** to see how much your scores go up.

I know you will like the stories in this book. And the exercises will help you read and write better.

Now . . . get ready for some *Travels.*

Burton Goodman

The Short Story—
Character, Plot, and Setting

Character: someone in a story. You can tell what the *character* is like by what the character says and does. The way a character looks may also be important.

Plot: what happens in a story. The first thing that happens in a story is the first thing in the *plot*. The last thing that happens in a story is the last thing in the plot.

Setting: where and when the story takes place. The *setting* is the time and place of the story.

1
Selling the Horse

by Don Juan Manuel

Before You Read

Before you read "Selling the Horse," go over the words below. Make sure you know what each word means. This will help you when you read the story.

smart: knowing a lot. People who are *smart* know a lot.

weak: not strong. Someone who is *weak* may fall down.

carry: to hold a thing and move it along. Mom asked me to *carry* the baby.

tired: needing rest or sleep. When you are *tired*, you want to rest.

Selling the Horse

by Don Juan Manuel

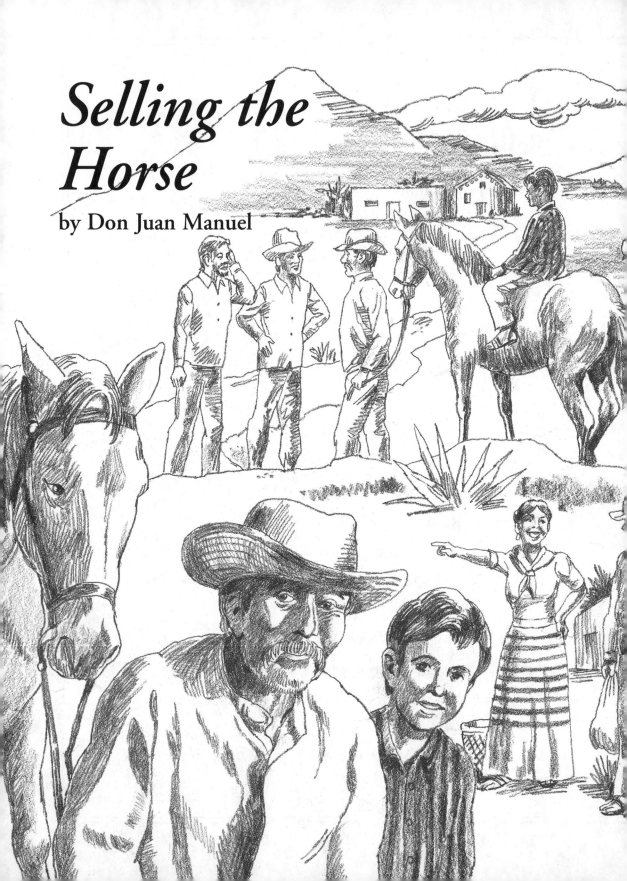

A farmer had a horse. It was a good horse. But it was getting old. The farmer said to himself, "Now is the time to sell my horse."

The farmer told his son, "Let us go into town. We can sell my horse there. Let us go today. We can leave now."

"All right," said the son. "I am ready. Let us go."

The father and the son left for the town. They walked along the road. The horse walked next to them.

Some people were coming down the road. The people were **returning** from the town. The people saw the farmer and his son. They saw the horse. They began to laugh.

The farmer said, "Why are you laughing at us? What is so funny?"

A man told the farmer, "You are not very smart. You are walking to town. So is your son. The horse is walking with you. You should *ride* on the horse. Or your son could ride. Why do you walk when you could ride?"

The farmer looked at his son. "What do you think, son?" he said.

"The man is right," said the boy.

"Well, then," the farmer said. "You can ride on the horse."

So the boy got on the horse. They went along that way. The boy rode on the back of the horse. The farmer walked next to them.

Soon they met some more people. The people looked at the farmer. They looked at the boy on the horse.

"Farmer," said a man. "You are old. You have worked hard for years. Your son is young. *You* should ride on the horse. You should let the boy walk. That is the right thing to do."

The farmer thought about that. Then he said, "All right."

So the boy got off the horse. The farmer **climbed** onto the horse. And they went along that way.

Soon they met more people. A woman said, "Farmer. This is **wrong.** Your son is young. He is weak. He is too weak to walk into town. You should let your son ride on the horse. He should ride with you."

So the boy got on the horse. The father and son *both* rode on the horse. And they went along that way.

Near town they met some more people. The people looked at the farmer and his son. They saw that the father and son were both riding the horse.

"Just look at that!" said one man. "See that poor horse. See how tired he is. He is an old horse. He cannot carry the farmer and his son. Oh, that poor horse!"

So the farmer and his son both got off the horse. They picked up the horse. They **lifted** him up high. They put him on their backs. And they carried the horse into town that way.

In town, people saw the farmer and his son.

"Look!" someone called out. "Look at this farmer and his son. They are *carrying* a horse!"

Everyone began to laugh.

The farmer and his son put the horse down on the ground.

The farmer turned to his son. The farmer said, "Son. What does this show?"

"I do not know," said the boy.

The farmer said, "It shows that you can never make everyone happy!"

TELL ABOUT THE STORY.

Put an X in the box next to the right answer. Each answer tells something (a *fact*) about the story.

1. The farmer wanted to
   - ☐ a. buy a horse.
   - ☐ b. sell his horse.
   - ☐ c. give his horse away.

2. A woman said the boy should ride because he was
   - ☐ a. weak.
   - ☐ b. good.
   - ☐ c. in a hurry.

3. The farmer and his son came into town
   - ☐ a. on the horse.
   - ☐ b. walking next to the horse.
   - ☐ c. with the horse on their backs.

4. When the farmer and his son got to town, people
   - ☐ a. laughed at them.
   - ☐ b. did not see them.
   - ☐ c. told them to go away.

END EACH LINE.

Finish the lines below. Fill in each empty space with one of the words in the box. Each word can be found in the story. There are five words and four empty spaces. This means that one word in the box will not be used. The first word has been done for you.

A long time ago horses were very

_____small_____. The first horses were
      1

only one to two feet _____.
                 2

But horses have gotten much bigger

over the _____. Many horses
         3

are six feet tall _____.
         4

years		small
	laugh	
today		high

NUMBER CORRECT ☐ X 5 = ☐ YOUR SCORE   NUMBER CORRECT ☐ X 5 = ☐ YOUR SCORE

Show WHAT WORDS MEAN.

The words below are printed in **dark letters** in the story. You may look back at these vocabulary words before you answer the questions. Put an X in the box next to the right answer.

1. The men were returning from town. The word *returning* means
    ☐ a. looking at.
    ☐ b. coming from.
    ☐ c. buying from.

2. The farmer climbed on the horse. The word *climbed* means
    ☐ a. got up on.
    ☐ b. fell down.
    ☐ c. talked about.

3. She said he was wrong to ride on the horse. Something that is *wrong* is
    ☐ a. very good.
    ☐ b. too old.
    ☐ c. not right.

4. They lifted the horse onto their backs. The word *lifted* means
    ☐ a. picked up.
    ☐ b. pushed away.
    ☐ c. tried hard.

Think ABOUT THE STORY.

Here is how to answer these questions. First think about what happened in the story. Then work out the right answers. This is called *critical thinking*.

1. In town, people laughed at the father and son because they were
    ☐ a. talking to the horse.
    ☐ b. feeding the horse.
    ☐ c. carrying the horse.

2. Which one is right?
    ☐ a. The son did not ride on the horse.
    ☐ b. The father did not ride on the horse.
    ☐ c. The farmer did what people told him to do.

3. The farmer wanted to sell the horse because it
    ☐ a. kicked a neighbor.
    ☐ b. was no longer young.
    ☐ c. had trouble walking.

4. At the end of the story, the farmer must have felt
    ☐ a. tired.
    ☐ b. worried.
    ☐ c. happy.

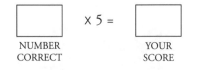

X 5 =

NUMBER CORRECT   YOUR SCORE

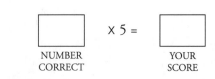

X 5 =

NUMBER CORRECT   YOUR SCORE

SPOT PARTS OF A STORY.

Stories have **characters**, a **plot**, and a **setting**. (See page 3.) Put an X in the box next to the right answer.

1. What happened first? (**Plot**)
   - ☐ a. A woman said the boy should ride.
   - ☐ b. The father and son left for town.
   - ☐ c. They put the horse on their backs.

2. What happened last? (**Plot**)
   - ☐ a. The father and son picked up the horse.
   - ☐ b. The father rode on the horse.
   - ☐ c. The son rode on the horse.

3. Which best tells about the farmer? (**Character**)
   - ☐ a. He listened to many people.
   - ☐ b. He did not listen to anyone.
   - ☐ c. He did not like his son.

4. Where does the story take place? (**Setting**)
   - ☐ a. on a farm
   - ☐ b. in and near a town
   - ☐ c. in a big city

THINK SOME MORE ABOUT THE STORY.

Your teacher might want you to write your answers.

- Many people told the farmer what to do. If you were the farmer, what would you have done?
- Why did the farmer say, "You can never make everyone happy"?
- Do you think the farmer sold his horse? Why?

Write your scores in the box below. Then write your scores on pages 122 and 123.

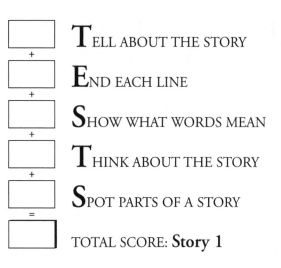

☐ +	**T**ELL ABOUT THE STORY
☐ +	**E**ND EACH LINE
☐ +	**S**HOW WHAT WORDS MEAN
☐ +	**T**HINK ABOUT THE STORY
☐ =	**S**POT PARTS OF A STORY
☐	TOTAL SCORE: **Story 1**

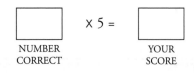

☐   x 5 =   ☐

NUMBER CORRECT   YOUR SCORE

2
The King and the Shoemaker

an old story

Before You Read

Before you read "The King and the Shoemaker," go over the words below. Make sure you know what each word means. This will help you when you read the story.

soldier: someone who fights for a king or others. The *soldier* had been fighting all day.

sword: something used for fighting. He killed three men with his *sword*.

sharp: having an edge that cuts easily. You can cut your hand on something that is *sharp*.

blade: the hard, cutting part of a sword. The *blade* of the sword was hard.

palace: the place where a king or queen lives. The queen lives in a *palace*.

The King and the Shoemaker

an old story

A king liked to **travel** around his land. He liked to see his people. He liked to talk to them. But he did not want them to know who he was.

So the king put on old clothes. He got on a horse. And he rode around his land.

One day the king was out riding. He came to a woods. There was a house by the woods. The house was very small. It was very old. It was nearly falling down.

The king heard a man's voice. The man was singing a song. The king listened to the words. This is what the man sang:

"I am old. That is so.
But wherever I go
I will find a way
To eat every day."

The king got off his horse. He walked to the house. He knocked on the door.

An old man came to the door.

"Yes?" said the old man.

The king said, "I have been riding all day. Now I am tired. May I rest here for a while?"

"Yes," said the old man. He did not know he was talking to the king.

"What do you do?" asked the king. "How do you make a living?"

"I am a shoemaker," said the old man. "I can fix shoes."

"You can fix shoes?" said the king. "Where do you work? Do people come to your house?"

"Oh, no," the shoemaker said. "I have a few **tools**. I take them with me. I go out every day. I stand by the side of the road. People pass by. I fix their shoes."

"I see," said the king. He thought about that. Then he said, "What if you could not fix shoes? How would you live?"

"Oh," said the old man. "I would find something to do."

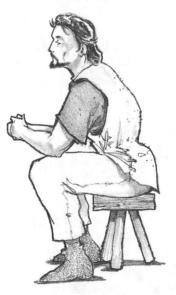

Then he began to sing:

"I am old. That is so.

But wherever I go

I will find a way

To eat every day."

The king said to himself, "We will see about *that!*" Then the king left the house.

The next morning a man came to the shoemaker's house.

The man told the shoemaker, "I come from the king. The king says this. To fix shoes, you must pay one piece of gold. You must pay it to the king."

"One piece of gold?" the shoemaker said. "But I do not have any gold."

"Then you cannot fix shoes," said the man.

That night the king put on old clothes. He got on a horse. He went to see the old man.

The king came near the house. He heard the shoemaker's voice. The old man was singing:

"I am old. That is so.

But wherever I go

I will find a way

To eat every day."

The king knocked on the door. The old man let him in.

The king said, "I was thinking about you. I know what the king said. Now you need gold to fix shoes. But you do not have any gold. What did you do? Were you able to eat?"

"Oh, yes," said the old man. "I thought for a long time. Then I said to myself, 'There are trees in the woods.' So I went into the woods. I cut down a tree. I **chopped** the tree into pieces. I sold the pieces for firewood. I made enough money to buy food for the day."

"I see," said the king.

The next day the shoemaker went into the woods. He cut down a tree.

A man rode up on a horse.

"You there!" said the man. "Did you cut down that tree?"

"I did," the shoemaker said.

"Come with me," said the man.

"But why?" said the shoemaker.

"I work for the king," said the man. "I watch over these woods. No one may cut down a tree. That is what the king said. He said that this morning."

"What will happen to me?" the shoemaker asked.

"You must work for the king. You must work for a week. You will work every day. You must work until five o'clock. Then you can go home."

The shoemaker asked, "Will they pay me for my work?"

"Yes," said the man. "But you must wait for a week."

"Wait for a week!" the shoemaker said. "But I need money for food!"

"There is nothing I can do," said the king's man. "Come with me now."

That night the king put on old clothes. He got on a horse. He went to see the old man.

The king came near the house. The king was surprised. The old man was singing. The king heard these words:

"I am old. That is so.

But wherever I go

I will find a way

To eat every day."

The king knocked on the door. The old man let the king in.

"What happened today?" asked the king.

"I cut down a tree," the shoemaker said. "The king's man saw me do that. He took me away."

"But why?" asked the king.

"No one may cut down a tree. The king said that today. Now I must work for the king. They will give me some money. But I must wait for a week."

"Wait for a week! Oh, you poor man!" said the king. "So you did not eat today!"

"Oh, yes," the shoemaker said. "I was able to eat. I got money for food."

"You did? Tell me how," said the king.

"They made me a soldier," the shoemaker said. "They gave me a sword. I put the sword in the holder. I marched up and down. I marched until five o'clock. Then I went home."

"Yes?" said the king.

"On the way home, I looked at the sword. It had a good blade. It was sharp. It could cut very well. I said to myself, 'I can sell this blade.' So I took the blade off the handle. I sold the blade. I bought food with the money I got."

The king was surprised. He said, "But what did you do with the sword? It did not have a blade."

"Oh," the shoemaker said. "I made a blade out of wood. I put the blade on the handle. I put the sword into the holder. No one can *see* the blade. It is in the holder."

"A blade made of wood!" said the king. "But what if they look at the blade?"

"We will see," said the old man.

The next day the shoemaker was marching around. One of the king's men came up to him.

"You there!" he said. "Come with me now. A man has done a bad thing. You must cut off his head!"

"Cut off his head?"

"Yes. Cut it off with your sword."

"I do not want to cut off a man's head!"

"The king says you must. You must cut off the man's head. Or you will lose your own head!"

They went to a place in the town. There were people all around. The people were waiting.

The king's man said, "See that man there. You must cut off his head. Use your sword. It is sharp. It has a sharp blade."

The man called out, "Do not cut off my head! *I did nothing bad!* Do not cut off my head!"

The shoemaker turned. The people were waiting.

The shoemaker said, "People. Listen to me. I believe this man. I believe what he says. But let us see. If he *did* something bad, let my blade be sharp—as it always is. If he did nothing bad, let my blade be made out of wood."

The shoemaker pulled out his sword.

It had turned to wood!

The people were **amazed.** They called out, "Let the man go! You must let the man go!"

So they let the man go.

The king was watching. He went up to the old man.

"Shoemaker," he said. "I am the king. I am also the man who was visiting you. I was wearing old clothes."

The shoemaker saw that the man was the king.

The king said, "Shoemaker. You are very clever. Someday I may need a man who is clever. Come to my palace. You may live there as long as you want."

The shoemaker said, "I will be happy to go."

So he went to the palace. And the shoemaker lived there the rest of his days.

Now and then people passed by the shoemaker's room. Sometimes they heard his voice. He was singing a song. The song went this way:

"I am old. That is so.
But wherever I go
I will find a way
To eat every day."

TELL ABOUT THE STORY.

Put an X in the box next to the right answer. Each answer tells something (a *fact*) about the story.

1. The king heard the shoemaker
   - ☐ a. calling for help.
   - ☐ b. singing a song.
   - ☐ c. talking to a friend.

2. The king's man said the shoemaker had to work for
   - ☐ a. a day.
   - ☐ b. a week.
   - ☐ c. a year.

3. The shoemaker sold the blade to get money for
   - ☐ a. food.
   - ☐ b. clothes.
   - ☐ c. shoes.

4. The king asked the shoemaker to
   - ☐ a. cut down a tree.
   - ☐ b. fix some shoes.
   - ☐ c. live at the palace.

END EACH LINE.

Finish the lines below. Fill in each empty space with one of the words in the box. Each word can be found in the story. There are five words and four empty spaces. This means that one word in the box will not be used.

A man named Thomas Beard was

the first American _____.
                           1

He went from house to house and

from town to _____. He
                  2

knocked on doors and told people

what he _____. Then he made
            3

shoes for anyone who gave him

_____.
    4

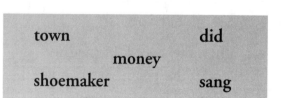

town		did
	money	
shoemaker		sang

☐ X 5 = ☐

NUMBER   YOUR
CORRECT   SCORE

☐ X 5 = ☐

NUMBER   YOUR
CORRECT   SCORE

31

SHOW WHAT WORDS MEAN.

The words below are printed in **dark letters** in the story. You may look back at these vocabulary words before you answer the questions. Put an X in the box next to the right answer.

1. The king liked to travel around his land. The word *travel* means to
   - ☐ a. stay at home.
   - ☐ b. go from place to place.
   - ☐ c. have fun.

2. The shoemaker used tools to fix shoes. People use *tools*
   - ☐ a. to walk on.
   - ☐ b. to wear.
   - ☐ c. to do work.

3. He chopped the tree into pieces. The word *chopped* means
   - ☐ a. cut up.
   - ☐ b. jumped on.
   - ☐ c. looked at.

4. When the sword "turned to wood," the people were amazed. The word *amazed* means very
   - ☐ a. glad.
   - ☐ b. sad.
   - ☐ c. surprised.

THINK ABOUT THE STORY.

Here is how to answer these questions. First think about what happened in the story. Then work out the right answers. This is called *critical thinking*.

1. The king put on old clothes because he
   - ☐ a. liked old clothes.
   - ☐ b. did not have new clothes.
   - ☐ c. did not want people to know who he was.

2. The king said the shoemaker had to
   - ☐ a. cut off a man's head.
   - ☐ b. fix the king's shoes.
   - ☐ c. sell some firewood.

3. When the shoemaker pulled out his sword, he knew that the blade was
   - ☐ a. very sharp.
   - ☐ b. going to break.
   - ☐ c. made of wood.

4. The shoemaker showed that he could
   - ☐ a. live for a long time without food.
   - ☐ b. find a way to eat every day.
   - ☐ c. make money by singing.

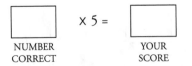

☐ X 5 = ☐

NUMBER
CORRECT

YOUR
SCORE

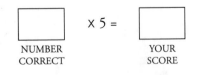

☐ X 5 = ☐

NUMBER
CORRECT

YOUR
SCORE

SPOT PARTS OF A STORY.

Stories have **characters**, a **plot**, and a **setting**. (See page 3.) Put an X in the box next to the right answer.

1. What happened first? **(Plot)**
   - ☐ a. The king asked the shoemaker how he made a living.
   - ☐ b. The shoemaker worked for the king.
   - ☐ c. The shoemaker cut down a tree.

2. What happened last? **(Plot)**
   - ☐ a. The king went to the shoemaker's house.
   - ☐ b. The shoemaker went to the palace.
   - ☐ c. The man said, "I did nothing bad."

3. Which best tells about the shoemaker? **(Character)**
   - ☐ a. He had a lot of money.
   - ☐ b. He was clever.
   - ☐ c. He was lazy.

4. When did the story take place? **(Setting)**
   - ☐ a. a year ago
   - ☐ b. five years ago
   - ☐ c. many years ago

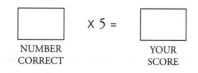

☐ X 5 = ☐

NUMBER CORRECT   YOUR SCORE

THINK SOME MORE ABOUT THE STORY.

Your teacher might want you to write your answers.

- Why did the king say the shoemaker had to pay gold to fix shoes?
- Why did the king say the shoemaker had to cut off a man's head?
- Why did the king ask the shoemaker to live at the palace?

Write your scores in the box below. Then write your scores on pages 122 and 123.

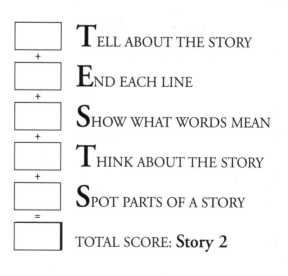

☐ **T**ELL ABOUT THE STORY
+
☐ **E**ND EACH LINE
+
☐ **S**HOW WHAT WORDS MEAN
+
☐ **T**HINK ABOUT THE STORY
+
☐ **S**POT PARTS OF A STORY
=
☐ TOTAL SCORE: **Story 2**

3
Across Time

by Lael J. Littke

Before You Read

Before you read "Across Time," go over the words below. Make sure you know what each word means. This will help you when you read the story.

hotel: a place to stay when you are on a trip. You pay for a room at a *hotel.*

inn: a small hotel. We stayed at an *inn* for one day.

fireplace: a place where you can make a fire. Our house has a stone *fireplace.*

log: a piece of wood from a tree. Put another *log* on the fire.

Across Time

by Lael J. Littke

Sarah looked out of the window of the car. It had started to rain. Now it was raining hard.

Sarah turned to her sister. "Karen," Sarah said. "We will have to stop soon. The rain is really coming down. It is hard for me to see."

Karen said, "Do you know where we are? Are we near Aunt Minna's house?"

"I do not know," Sarah said. "I just visited her once. That was a long time ago."

Sarah **stared** out of the window. She said, "I do not see any of the things she said to look for."

Now it was getting dark. Sarah felt cold. "We must stop somewhere," she said. "We will have to stay there for the night."

"You are right," Karen said. "I am getting tired. You must be tired too. And Aunt Minna does not **expect** us tonight."

Karen smiled. She said, "It would be great if there was a hotel just ahead. A big, beautiful place. One with very good food."

Sarah laughed. "No way!" she said. "But there *is* a little inn. It is around the next turn."

Karen was surprised. She stopped looking out of the window. She turned to her sister. "How do you know *that?*" Karen asked.

Sarah said, "I—I—I am not sure. I just *know* it is there. It is on top of a hill. The inn is white. It has a blue door. There is a big tree behind it."

Karen laughed. But then she saw a sign. The sign said *INN AHEAD.*

Karen looked to the right. There was an inn. It was on top of a hill! Behind it was a tree!

Sarah drove to the front of the inn. It had a blue door!

Karen looked at Sarah. "Tell me," Karen said. "How did you know the inn was here?"

Sarah said, "I really do not know. I have never been here before. Maybe I saw it years ago. Or I might have seen it in a picture. That must be it."

Karen suddenly felt frightened. "Sarah," she said. "Let us go. We can find some other place."

"No," Sarah said. "It is raining too hard. This will be all right."

Sarah knocked on the door.

A woman came to the door. She had long, gray hair. She looked very old.

"Come in," she said. "I have been waiting for you."

"Waiting for us?" Karen said. "What do you mean?"

The woman smiled. She said, "People come here when it is raining hard. Then they will stay at an old inn."

The woman let them in. She said, "My name is Mrs. Burns."

She pointed to some steps.

"Go up those stairs," she said. "You will find two rooms at the top. You can stay there tonight. You must be hungry. I will make something to eat. I will call you when it is ready."

The sisters walked up the stairs. Sarah went to one room. She started to open the door. Suddenly she stopped.

"What is the matter?" Karen said.

Sarah said, "It is strange. But I know what this room looks like. There is a fireplace in the room. There is a picture over the fireplace. There is a woman in the picture.

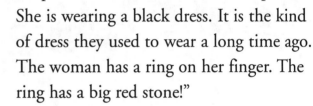

She is wearing a black dress. It is the kind of dress they used to wear a long time ago. The woman has a ring on her finger. The ring has a big red stone!"

They opened the door.

There was a fireplace in the room. Over the fireplace was a picture. A woman was wearing a black dress. On her finger was a ring. The ring had a big red stone.

Sarah and Karen looked at each other. They did not know what to think.

Just then they heard Mrs. Burns's voice. "The food is ready," she said.

The food was hot. It was very good. Sarah and Karen ate. Mrs. Burns talked about the inn.

She said, "This inn is very old. It has been here for more than 100 years."

Sarah said, "Who is the woman in the picture?"

Mrs. Burns smiled. "Why, dear, that was *me*. It was me many years ago. I was much younger then. Did you see the ring on my finger?"

"Yes," Karen said.

"I gave that ring to a woman. Her name was Judith. She was going to marry my son."

Mrs. Burns stopped talking. She looked very sad.

Mrs. Burns went on. "But my son died suddenly. Judith **disappeared.** And so did the ring. No one has ever seen them again."

Karen asked, "Did the ring mean much to you?"

"Oh, yes," said Mrs. Burns. "It has been in my family for years. I would love to get it back."

Sarah said, "It is getting late. And we must leave early tomorrow. We are looking for our aunt. Her name is Minna Todd. Do you know her?"

"No," said Mrs. Burns. "But you will find a store along the road ahead. Ask at the store. They know everyone around here."

"We will do that in the morning," Karen said. "It is getting late. We should really say good night."

Sarah was very tired. She fell fast asleep that night. In the middle of the night, Sarah heard a voice.

"Judith," said the voice. "Can you hear me, Judith?"

Sarah looked up. There was a woman in the room! She was the woman in the picture! Mrs. Burns had said she was that woman.

Sarah said, "I can hear you. But my name is not Judith. My name is Sarah."

The woman said, "I knew you would come back. I am so glad that you did. I have been waiting for you. I have waited a long, long time."

The woman came closer to the bed. "Where is the ring, Judith?" she asked. "Tell me. Where is the ring?"

"What ring?" Sarah said. "And my name is not Judith. It is Sarah!"

"Think!" said the woman. "Where is the ring?"

Suddenly Sarah got up. She moved to the fireplace. She reached up to the picture. She put her hand behind it. She found a place there. She pulled something out.

"Here is the ring," Sarah said.

The sisters got up early the next morning. Karen said, "I was so tired. I slept like a log. Did you sleep well, Sarah?"

"Yes," Sarah said. "But I had a strange dream. I dreamed I was someone named Judith."

"Judith?" said Karen. "Mrs. Burns told us about someone named Judith."

"Yes," Sarah said. "Mrs. Burns was in my dream too. She was the woman in the picture."

Karen laughed. "You sure can **imagine** things, Sarah," she said. "Now we should be going. Let us see if we can find Mrs. Burns."

Sarah and Karen went downstairs. They looked around. But Mrs. Burns was not there.

The sisters put some money on the table. Then they got into the car. They drove away from the inn. They found the store Mrs. Burns told them about.

They asked the man there about Minna Todd.

"Minna Todd?" he said. "I know where she lives. It is not far from here."

He told them the way to go. Then he asked, "Did you stay at the inn?"

"Yes," Karen said.

The man said, "Then you met Mrs. Burns. It is funny. She came by early today. She said she was going away. She said she did not have to stay here anymore."

"Going away?" Sarah said.

"Yes," said the man. "And she was wearing a ring. I never saw her wear it before. The ring had a big red stone."

"A ring with a big red stone!" Sarah said.

Sarah started to say something. She was going to say, "I gave Mrs. Burns the ring in my dream." Then Sarah stopped. It was all too hard to believe. She did not say a word.

TELL ABOUT THE STORY.

Put an X in the box next to the right answer. Each answer tells something (a *fact*) about the story.

1. The sisters stopped at the inn because
   - ☐ a. Aunt Minna said to stay there.
   - ☐ b. they heard it was good.
   - ☐ c. it was raining and they were tired.

2. The inn was
   - ☐ a. a big, beautiful place.
   - ☐ b. on a hill by a tree.
   - ☐ c. far away from the road.

3. The woman in the picture was wearing
   - ☐ a. a short coat.
   - ☐ b. a red dress.
   - ☐ c. a red ring.

4. Sarah thought she dreamed that
   - ☐ a. someone kept calling her Judith.
   - ☐ b. she met Aunt Minna.
   - ☐ c. she went to a store.

END EACH LINE.

Finish the lines below. Fill in each empty space with one of the words in the box. Each word can be found in the story. There are five words and four empty spaces. This means that one word in the box will not be used.

Long before there were hotels, people stayed at _____. The inns were not very _____. They had just a few _____. You got a bed for the night and something to _____.

1

2

3

4

> picture   inns
>   eat
> rooms   big

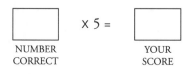

NUMBER CORRECT   x 5 =   YOUR SCORE

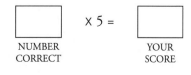

NUMBER CORRECT   x 5 =   YOUR SCORE

47

SHOW WHAT WORDS MEAN.

The words below are printed in **dark letters** in the story. You may look back at these vocabulary words before you answer the questions. Put an X in the box next to the right answer.

1. Sarah stared out of the window. The word *stared* means
   - ☐ a. looked at closely.
   - ☐ b. did not see.
   - ☐ c. opened up.

2. Aunt Minna did not expect them that night. The word *expect* means to
   - ☐ a. think someone is coming.
   - ☐ b. like someone very much.
   - ☐ c. tell someone to go away.

3. The ring disappeared years ago. Something that has *disappeared*
   - ☐ a. is small.
   - ☐ b. cannot be seen.
   - ☐ c. can easily be seen.

4. Karen said, "You sure can imagine things." When you *imagine* things you
   - ☐ a. lose them.
   - ☐ b. look for them.
   - ☐ c. make them up.

THINK ABOUT THE STORY.

Here is how to answer these questions. First think about what happened in the story. Then work out the right answers. This is called *critical thinking*.

1. It was strange that Sarah
   - ☐ a. could not see in the rain.
   - ☐ b. was very hungry.
   - ☐ c. knew there was an inn just ahead.

2. It was also strange that Sarah
   - ☐ a. knew what the room looked like.
   - ☐ b. fell fast asleep.
   - ☐ c. was going to visit her aunt.

3. Which one is true?
   - ☐ a. The inn was 200 years old.
   - ☐ b. Mrs. Burns said, "I have been waiting for you."
   - ☐ c. Karen did not sleep well.

4. We can guess that Mrs. Burns left the inn because she
   - ☐ a. had to buy food.
   - ☐ b. was too old to work there.
   - ☐ c. got the ring she wanted so much.

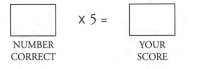

NUMBER CORRECT   × 5 =   YOUR SCORE

NUMBER CORRECT   × 5 =   YOUR SCORE

Spot Parts of a Story.

Stories have **characters**, a **plot**, and a **setting.** (See page 3.) Put an X in the box next to the right answer.

1. What happened first? (**Plot**)
   - ☐ a. Mrs. Burns made food.
   - ☐ b. The sisters came to an inn.
   - ☐ c. The sisters saw a sign that read *INN AHEAD.*

2. What happened last? (**Plot**)
   - ☐ a. Mrs. Burns made food for Sarah and Karen.
   - ☐ b. The man said Mrs. Burns was wearing a ring.
   - ☐ c. Mrs. Burns told them about Judith.

3. Which best tells about Mrs. Burns? (**Character**)
   - ☐ a. She looked very old.
   - ☐ b. She knew Aunt Minna.
   - ☐ c. She had short, dark hair.

4. Where does most of the story take place? (**Setting**)
   - ☐ a. in a store along the road
   - ☐ b. at Aunt Minna's house
   - ☐ c. in an inn

Think Some More About the Story.

Your teacher might want you to write your answers.

- Why do you think the story is called "Across Time"?
- Why do you think Mrs. Burns was going away?
- Sarah thought, "It was all too hard to believe." What did she mean?

Write your scores in the box below. Then write your scores on pages 122 and 123.

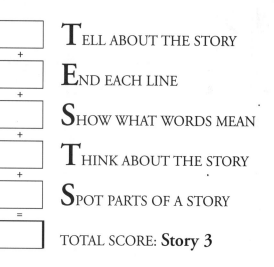

☐ +	**T**ELL ABOUT THE STORY
☐ +	**E**ND EACH LINE
☐ +	**S**HOW WHAT WORDS MEAN
☐ +	**T**HINK ABOUT THE STORY
☐ =	**S**POT PARTS OF A STORY
☐	TOTAL SCORE: **Story 3**

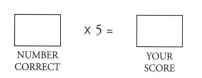

☐   X 5 =   ☐

NUMBER CORRECT   YOUR SCORE

4

Morning Sunshine

a story from West Africa

Before You Read

Before you read "Morning Sunshine," go over the words below. Make sure you know what each word means. This will help you when you read the story.

shopkeeper: someone who has a store that he or she runs. The *shopkeeper* works in her store all day.

alive: living. Rain keeps the flowers *alive*.

dead: not living. I knew the bird was *dead* because it did not move.

tear: a drop of water that comes from the eye. She was so sad that *tear* after *tear* fell from her eyes.

plant: to put something in the ground so that it will grow. She wanted to *plant* a tree in the garden.

Morning Sunshine

a story from West Africa

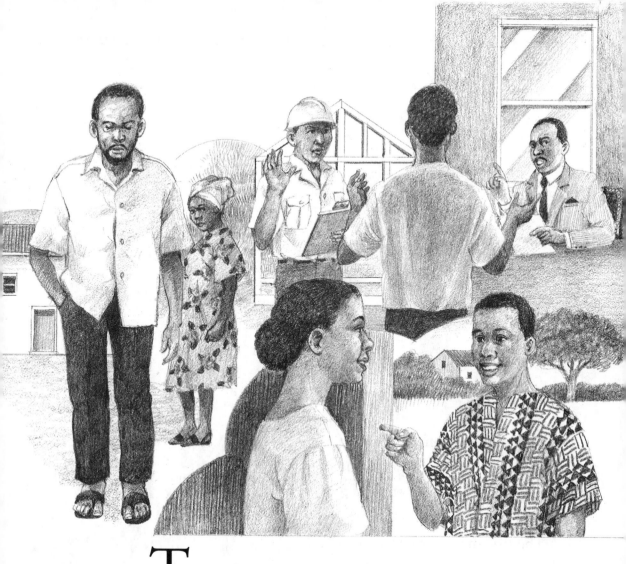

There once was a man. His name was Aziz. Aziz lived in Kenda. That is a town in West Africa.

Aziz had a daughter. She was very pretty. She had a beautiful smile. She smiled all the time. So everyone called her "Morning Sunshine."

Yes, Morning Sunshine was beautiful. She also was wise. And she was very kind.

Many young men lived in Kenda. Many of them fell in love with Morning Sunshine. They all wanted to marry her.

Morning Sunshine liked three men very much. Each man came from a good family. Each man seemed very nice. Which man should she marry?

The first man was named Dema. He was a builder. He had built many houses. He told Morning Sunshine, "Please marry me. I love you very much. I will build you a big house. It will have many rooms. You will have a big garden. Please marry me."

The second man was named Hassa. He owned a bank. He said to Morning Sunshine, "Please marry me. I will give

you a lot of money. You will have beautiful clothes. You will eat the best food. You will live like a queen. Please marry me."

The third man was a shopkeeper. His name was Ali. He said to Morning Sunshine, "Please marry me. I love you most of all. I am not rich. But I have enough money. I will try to give you whatever you want. I just want to make you happy."

What should she do? Morning Sunshine did not know.

She wanted to marry the right man. She **spoke** to her father. He said, "I will help you, Morning Sunshine. I will help you **choose** the right man."

Aziz thought for a long time. Then he said, "Morning Sunshine. This is what you must do. Stay in the house. Do not go outside. Do not talk to anyone. Do not let anyone see you."

Morning Sunshine stayed in her house. She did not go outside. She did not let anyone see her.

One day Aziz left the house and went into town. People saw Aziz. They said to him, "Aziz. Where is Morning Sunshine? We have not seen her for a week. Is she all right?"

Aziz looked very sad. He said, "Morning Sunshine is not well. She is **sick.** She is very, very sick."

Aziz waited two more days. Then he sent for a friend. The friend's name was Omar.

Aziz said, "Omar, my friend. I need your help. Please do this for me. Go into town. Look very sad. Say that Morning Sunshine is dead. Do not let anyone know she is still alive."

"I will do that," said Omar.

"Thank you," said Aziz. "Please do one more thing. Find these three men. They are Dema, Hassa, and Ali. Here is what to tell them."

Aziz told his friend what to say.

Omar went into town. He looked very sad. People said, "Omar. What is the matter?"

Omar said softly, "Morning Sunshine is dead."

Then Omar went to find Dema. He found him in a field. His men were building a house. Dema was watching the men work.

Omar said, "My name is Omar. I come from Aziz. Morning Sunshine is dead."

"Yes," said Dema. "I have heard. Word came from the town."

Omar said, "Aziz said you loved Morning Sunshine. He said you loved her very much. Soon they will put Morning Sunshine in the ground. The family wants to buy a stone. They want to put it on that ground. Morning Sunshine's name will be on the stone. People will see the stone. They will see her name. They will remember Morning Sunshine."

"Yes?" said Dema.

Omar went on. "But the family is poor. They cannot buy the stone. You have a lot of money. Aziz wants to know this. Can you give him some money for a stone?"

"Ha!" said Dema. He got very angry. "What is Morning Sunshine to me? She was not my wife! I have no money for Aziz!"

He sent Omar away.

Omar went to find Hassa. He found Hassa at his bank.

Omar said, "My name is Omar. I come from Aziz. Morning Sunshine is dead."

"Yes," said Hassa. "I have heard."

Omar said, "The family is poor. They want to buy some flowers. They will put them on the ground where Morning Sunshine lies. Aziz said you loved Morning Sunshine. He says you loved her very much. Will you give Aziz money for flowers?"

"Give Aziz money for flowers?" Hassa looked surprised. "Why should I give money to Aziz? Morning Sunshine is dead. What is she to me? She was not my wife. I have no money for Aziz."

And he sent Omar away.

Omar went to find Ali. He found him in his shop.

Omar said, "My name is Omar. I come from Aziz. Morning Sunshine is dead."

"Yes," said Ali. "I have heard." He **wiped** a tear from his eye.

Omar said, "The family is poor. They want to plant a little tree. They will put it in the ground where Morning Sunshine lies. Can you give Aziz some money for a tree?"

"Money for a tree?" said Ali. "Yes! Aziz shall have money for a tree. And for flowers and a stone! For if Morning Sunshine had lived, I am sure she would have been my wife."

The next day Ali brought the money to Aziz's house. And who was waiting at the door? It was Morning Sunshine herself. She was not dead after all!

Aziz was standing at Morning Sunshine's side.

Aziz turned to Morning Sunshine. He said, "Morning Sunshine, Ali is the right man for you."

Ali was so happy he could not say a word. He just smiled.

Morning Sunshine smiled back. And, you know, she had a beautiful smile.

"Yes, father," she said. "Ali is the right man for me!"

TELL ABOUT THE STORY.

Put an X in the box next to the right answer. Each answer tells something (a *fact*) about the story.

1. Aziz said he would help Morning Sunshine
   - ☐ a. make a lot of money.
   - ☐ b. find new friends.
   - ☐ c. find the right man.

2. The builder said he would give Morning Sunshine
   - ☐ a. a big house with a big garden.
   - ☐ b. a new car.
   - ☐ c. anything she wanted.

3. Omar told people that Morning Sunshine
   - ☐ a. had moved away.
   - ☐ b. was resting at home.
   - ☐ c. was dead.

4. Omar asked the banker for money to buy
   - ☐ a. food.
   - ☐ b. flowers.
   - ☐ c. beautiful clothes.

END EACH LINE.

Finish the lines below. Fill in each empty space with one of the words in the box. Each word can be found in the story. There are five words and four empty spaces. This means that one word in the box will not be used.

A very long time ago, people did

not need _____. This is
         1

because the people grew their own

_____. They hunted animals
      2

to _____. And they built their
        3

own _____.
        4

soon	**food**
money	
houses	**eat**

 x 5 =

NUMBER   YOUR
CORRECT   SCORE

NUMBER   YOUR
CORRECT   SCORE

SHOW WHAT WORDS MEAN.

The words below are printed in **dark letters** in the story. You may look back at these vocabulary words before you answer the questions. Put an X in the box next to the right answer.

1. Morning Sunshine spoke to her father. The word *spoke* means
   - ☐ a. laughed at.
   - ☐ b. talked to.
   - ☐ c. gave money to.

2. He wanted her to choose the right man. The word *choose* means
   - ☐ a. pick.
   - ☐ b. keep.
   - ☐ c. need.

3. Aziz said that Morning Sunshine was sick. When you are *sick,* you are
   - ☐ a. young.
   - ☐ b. happy.
   - ☐ c. not well.

4. Ali wiped a tear from his eye. The word *wiped* means
   - ☐ a. looked at.
   - ☐ b. smiled.
   - ☐ c. rubbed away.

THINK ABOUT THE STORY.

Here is how to answer these questions. First think about what happened in the story. Then work out the right answers. This is called *critical thinking.*

1. Aziz said that Morning Sunshine was dead because he wanted to
   - ☐ a. get money.
   - ☐ b. make people sad.
   - ☐ c. see what the three men would do.

2. Ali was willing to give Aziz money because Ali
   - ☐ a. loved Morning Sunshine.
   - ☐ b. had so much money.
   - ☐ c. did not believe Morning Sunshine was dead.

3. At the end of the story, Ali was
   - ☐ a. sad.
   - ☐ b. tired.
   - ☐ c. surprised and happy.

4. We can guess that Morning Sunshine
   - ☐ a. married Hassa.
   - ☐ b. married Ali.
   - ☐ c. did not get married after all.

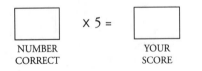

NUMBER CORRECT   × 5 =   YOUR SCORE

NUMBER CORRECT   × 5 =   YOUR SCORE

SPOT PARTS OF A STORY.

Stories have **characters**, a **plot**, and a **setting**. (See page 3.) Put an X in the box next to the right answer.

1. What happened last? (**Plot**)
   - ☐ a. Omar asked the banker for money.
   - ☐ b. Dema asked Morning Sunshine to marry him.
   - ☐ c. Ali brought money to Aziz.

2. Which best tells about Morning Sunshine? (**Character**)
   - ☐ a. She did not like to smile.
   - ☐ b. She was pretty and wise.
   - ☐ c. She loved money more than anything.

3. Which best tells about Aziz? (**Character**)
   - ☐ a. He helped Morning Sunshine.
   - ☐ b. He did not care about Morning Sunshine.
   - ☐ c. He had no friends.

4. Where does the story take place? (**Setting**)
   - ☐ a. in a big city
   - ☐ b. in a town in West Africa
   - ☐ c. in the United States

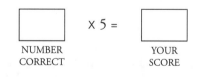

NUMBER CORRECT   X 5 =   YOUR SCORE

THINK SOME MORE ABOUT THE STORY.

Your teacher might want you to write your answers.

- Why did many men want to marry Morning Sunshine?
- Why didn't Dema and Hassa give money to Omar?
- Do you think Ali was the right man for Morning Sunshine? Why?

Write your scores in the box below. Then write your scores on pages 122 and 123.

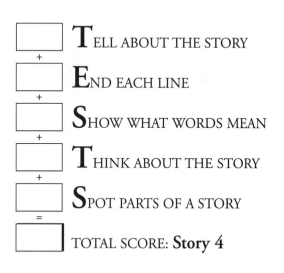

- **T**ELL ABOUT THE STORY
- +
- **E**ND EACH LINE
- +
- **S**HOW WHAT WORDS MEAN
- +
- **T**HINK ABOUT THE STORY
- +
- **S**POT PARTS OF A STORY
- =
- TOTAL SCORE: **Story 4**

5
Two Who Flew

a Greek myth

Before You Read

Before you read "Two Who Flew," go over the words below. Make sure you know what each word means. This will help you when you read the story.

island: land that has water all around it. We needed a boat to get to the *island.*

beast: a big animal that people are afraid of. Everyone ran from the *beast.*

wax: something that is hard when cold and soft when warm. The hot sun made the *wax* candles soft.

melts: makes soft or turns to water. When ice *melts,* it becomes water.

Two Who Flew

a Greek myth

A myth is a very old story. It was made up a long time ago. It has lasted through the years.

There are many myths. Some tell about people who were great. They might have been very strong. They might have been very smart. They might have done wonderful things.

This is a Greek myth. It is about a man. Daedalus (DED'•A•LUS) was his name.

Daedalus was very smart. He liked to build things. He could make anything.

Crete is an island. There is water all around it. The king of Crete needed help. He did not know what to do. Then he said to himself, "Maybe Daedalus can help me." So the king sent for him.

Daedalus got on a boat. He went to Crete with his son. Icarus (IK′•A•RUS) was the boy's name.

Daedalus met the king. The king said, "Daedalus, I am glad you are here. I have heard about you. I know you are smart. You can build anything."

Daedalus said, "How can I help you? What do you want me to do?"

The king said, "There is a beast. It lives here in Crete. It has hurt many people. We cannot kill this beast. It is much too big. It is much too strong. Can you build something to hold in this beast? Can you build something that will keep it away from people?"

Daedalus said, "Let me think."

"I will pay you well," said the king. "I will give you a lot of gold."

Daedalus thought for a while. Then he said, "I know what to do."

Daedalus built something. He called it a maze. The maze was very big. It went around and around. It went in and out. There were many different ways to go in the maze.

The beast saw the maze. It wondered what it was. It went into the maze. The beast went around and around. It went this way and that. It could not find the way out of the maze.

The king was happy.

Daedalus said, "Now please give me my gold."

The king laughed. He said, "The beast cannot get out. It goes around and around. I will not give you any gold. If I do, you will leave Crete. You will go far away. You will help someone else. No. I will lock you in a room. I will keep you there. I may need your help again."

The king's men locked Daedalus in a room. They put him there with his son. But Daedalus was very smart. He could make anything. He made a key. He waited until night. Then Daedalus used the key to open the door. He **escaped** from the room. He and Icarus got away. They **hid** on the island. The king could not find them.

The king was angry. He told his men, "You must **search** every boat that leaves Crete. Do it with care. Make sure that Daedalus is not on any boat."

The king thought to himself, "Daedalus is smart. But he will not get away. He will never leave this island."

Daedalus wanted to leave Crete. But how could he do that? Crete is an island. There is water all around it.

One day, Daedalus was looking at the sky. He was watching some birds. Daedalus said to his son, "Icarus, see those birds. They are free. They can fly anywhere. I wish we could fly. We could fly away from this place. We could leave this island. The king could not stop us."

"That is so," Icarus said. "But we are not birds. We cannot fly."

Daedalus kept watching the birds. He saw how the birds flew. He saw the **shape** of their wings. He saw how the wings moved.

Then Daedalus said to his son, "Let us go into the hills. Birds build their nests in the hills. We will find feathers there. I need many feathers. I want to make wings."

They went into the hills. They found feathers there. Some feathers were big. Others were small. The father and son got many feathers.

Yes, Daedalus was smart. He could build anything. He put the feathers together with wax. The wax held them in place. He made a big pair of wings.

Daedalus put the wings around his back. He tied the wings to his arms. He moved his arms up and down. He beat the air with his wings. That was what the birds did. Daedalus moved up into the air. And soon he was flying!

Daedalus made another pair of wings. "Here, Icarus," he said. "These are for you."

Icarus put the wings on his back. He tied the wings to his arms.

Then Daedalus said, "With these wings we can fly. We can fly like the birds. We can fly anywhere. With these wings we can leave Crete. We can fly over the water. We can fly back to our home!"

Icarus smiled. He was happy to go.

Daedalus said, "I will go first. Let me lead the way. You follow me."

They got ready to leave. Daedalus said, "Icarus, my son. Listen to me. Listen very well. Do not fly too low. But do not fly too high. Stay far away from the sun. Just follow me."

"I will," said the boy.

Daedalus said, "We must wait for a wind."

Soon the winds began to blow. They began to blow hard. Daedalus said, "This is a good time to go."

Daedalus moved his arms up and down. His wings beat the air. Icarus did the same thing. Soon father and son were flying through the air.

Daedalus led the way. Icarus followed him. They flew over the water! They flew for a long time.

"Flying is fun!" Icarus cried. He began to fly fast. He flew faster and faster.

"Yes. Flying is fun!" Icarus called out. He flew higher and higher and higher.

"Wait! Icarus!" Daedalus called. "You are flying too high!" But the boy was too far away. He could not hear his father.

Icarus flew closer to the sun. It was hot near the sun. The feathers on his wings were held together by wax. The wax began to melt. The feathers fell out. The wings did not work! The boy began to fall!

Down Icarus fell. Down, down, down went the boy.
Poor Daedalus watched. There was nothing he could do.
The boy hit the water. And then he was gone!

Daedalus flew on. But he was very sad. He had lost his
son. The fun of flying was gone.

Soon Daedalus reached home. He took off his wings. He
put them away. And he never flew again.

Tell About the Story.

Put an X in the box next to the right answer. Each answer tells something (a *fact*) about the story.

1. The king asked Daedalus to make something that would
   - ☐ a. kill the beast.
   - ☐ b. hold in the beast.
   - ☐ c. make the beast go away.

2. Daedalus left Crete by
   - ☐ a. taking a boat.
   - ☐ b. flying in an airplane.
   - ☐ c. flying like a bird.

3. Daedalus told Icarus to
   - ☐ a. fly very low.
   - ☐ b. stay far away from the sun.
   - ☐ c. fly as fast as he could.

4. Icarus fell
   - ☐ a. into the water.
   - ☐ b. down a hill.
   - ☐ c. off a boat.

End Each Line.

Finish the lines below. Fill in each empty space with one of the words in the box. Each word can be found in the story. There are five words and four empty spaces. This means that one word in the box will not be used.

Wilbur and Orville Wright wanted

to _____. They worked on an
      1

airplane for seven _____. In
                        2

1903 they were ready to see if it

_____. It did—Wilbur flew
    3

120 feet through the _____.
                          4

birds	**air**
worked	
fly	**years**

NUMBER CORRECT X 5 = YOUR SCORE

NUMBER CORRECT X 5 = YOUR SCORE

75

Show what words mean.

The words below are printed in **dark letters** in the story. You may look back at these vocabulary words before you answer the questions. Put an X in the box next to the right answer.

1. Daedalus escaped from the room. The word *escaped* means
    □ a. got out of.
    □ b. knew about.
    □ c. looked into.

2. Daedalus and Icarus hid on the island. The word *hid* means
    □ a. asked for help.
    □ b. looked for friends.
    □ c. went where it is hard to be seen.

3. The king told his men to search every boat. The word *search* means to
    □ a. go far away.
    □ b. open and close.
    □ c. try to find by looking.

4. He saw the shape of the birds' wings. The *shape* of something is the
    □ a. way it looks.
    □ b. way it sounds.
    □ c. way it smells.

Think about the story.

Here is how to answer these questions. First think about what happened in the story. Then work out the right answers. This is called *critical thinking*.

1. Daedalus learned how to fly by
    □ a. reading books.
    □ b. watching birds.
    □ c. talking to other people.

2. Which one is true?
    □ a. The king gave Daedalus gold.
    □ b. The beast got out of the maze.
    □ c. Daedalus came home alone.

3. At the end of the story, Daedalus was
    □ a. happy because he could fly.
    □ b. sad because his son was gone.
    □ c. angry because the wings did not work.

4. The story shows that Icarus
    □ a. did not fly high enough.
    □ b. did not fly fast enough.
    □ c. should have listened to his father.

X 5 =

NUMBER CORRECT   YOUR SCORE

X 5 =

NUMBER CORRECT   YOUR SCORE

SPOT PARTS OF A STORY.

Stories have **characters**, a **plot**, and a **setting**. (See page 3.) Put an X in the box next to the right answer.

1. What happened first? (**Plot**)
   - ☐ a. The beast went into the maze.
   - ☐ b. Daedalus went to Crete.
   - ☐ c. Daedalus made some wings.

2. What happened last? (**Plot**)
   - ☐ a. They put Daedalus in a room.
   - ☐ b. Icarus fell into the water.
   - ☐ c. Icarus began to fly higher.

3. Which best tells about Daedalus? (**Character**)
   - ☐ a. He could make anything.
   - ☐ b. He did not like to build things.
   - ☐ c. He did not want to leave Crete.

4. When does the story take place? (**Setting**)
   - ☐ a. today
   - ☐ b. last year
   - ☐ c. a long time ago

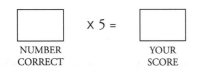

NUMBER CORRECT   X 5 =   YOUR SCORE

THINK SOME MORE ABOUT THE STORY.

Your teacher might want you to write your answers.

- Why do you think Daedalus waited for a wind before he and Icarus started to fly?
- What if Icarus had stayed behind his father in the air? How do you think the story would have ended?
- Why didn't Daedalus ever fly again?

Write your scores in the box below. Then write your scores on pages 122 and 123.

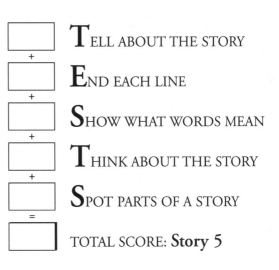

☐ **T**ELL ABOUT THE STORY
+
☐ **E**ND EACH LINE
+
☐ **S**HOW WHAT WORDS MEAN
+
☐ **T**HINK ABOUT THE STORY
+
☐ **S**POT PARTS OF A STORY
=
☐ TOTAL SCORE: **Story 5**

77

6
The Queen's Garden

by Ellen C. Babbitt

Before You Read

Before you read "The Queen's Garden," go over the words below. Make sure you know what each word means. This will help you when you read the story.

pearls: small, round stones. She was wearing *pearls* around her neck.

guard: someone who watches over, or takes care of, someone. There was always a *guard* near the queen.

woke: stopped sleeping. He *woke* up when he heard a loud noise.

warned: told to be careful. The queen *warned* the monkey and then let it go.

The Queen's Garden

by Ellen C. Babbitt

A queen had a beautiful garden. The garden was filled with flowers. There were many tall trees in the garden. Birds sang in the garden all day. And monkeys jumped and played in the trees.

The queen loved her beautiful garden. She loved to look at the flowers. She loved to hear the birds singing. She loved to walk by the trees.

There was a lake near the garden. The queen often sat by the lake. She looked out at the water.

One day the queen took a walk. The day was warm. The road was long. The queen got tired. She went back to the palace to rest.

The queen rested for a while. Then she said to herself, "I will go to my garden. I will sit under a tree. Then I will swim in the lake. That will be very nice."

She **prepared** to swim in the lake. Then she went to the garden.

The queen sat in a chair. It was under a tree. She looked out at the lake. She sat for some time. Then she got up to swim.

The queen was wearing some pearls. She reached up to her neck. She took off the pearls. She put them down on the chair.

"Guard!" called the queen.

A guard ran up. "Yes, queen," he said.

"Watch this string of pearls," said the queen. "I am going to swim."

"Very good," said the guard.

The queen went to the lake.

The guard looked at the pearls. They were bright in the sun.

A monkey sat in the tree by the chair. It watched all of this. It heard what they said.

The monkey thought, "She is the queen. He is a guard. That thing on the chair is a string of pearls."

The monkey looked at the pearls. Oh, my, they were bright!

The monkey thought, "I like those pearls very much! I want those pearls very much. I must have those pearls!"

The monkey looked at the guard. The guard watched the pearls.

The day was hot. The guard was tired. The monkey thought, "I will keep watching the guard. He may fall asleep. If he falls asleep, I will get the pearls."

The guard closed his eyes. He soon fell asleep.

The monkey jumped down from the tree. It picked up the pearls. It ran back up the tree.

The monkey put the pearls around its neck. The pearls looked very good. The monkey was happy.

There was a hole in the tree. The monkey put the pearls into the hole. "They will be **safe** in the tree," the monkey said.

Soon the guard woke up. He looked at the chair. The pearls were gone!

The guard called out, "A man has run off with the queen's string of pearls! A man has run off with the queen's string of pearls!"

Guards hurried there from every side. Just then the queen came back. She had finished her swim.

"Where are my pearls?" she asked the guard.

"My queen," said the guard. "I was sitting right there. I was watching your pearls. But I closed my eyes. I fell asleep. When I woke up, the pearls were gone."

"Gone?" said the queen.

She turned to the guards. "Look everywhere," she said. "Find the man who took the pearls. Then bring that man to me."

Two days went by. The guards looked everywhere. They told the queen, "Your pearls are gone. We cannot find them anywhere. We cannot find the man who took them."

"What?" said the queen. "You cannot find the man? How can that be? There is a fence around the garden. Guards stand by the fence all day. He could not get away."

"Yes," said the guards. "But still we cannot find the man."

The queen thought and thought. Then she said, "There are many monkeys in my garden. **Perhaps** a monkey took the pearls."

She turned to the guards. "Go," she said. "Make many strings of pearls. But make them out of glass. Wait until the sun goes down. Put the pearls around the garden. We will see what happens then."

The guards made many pearls of glass. That night they put them in the garden.

The pearls were bright. The monkeys saw the strings of pearls. The monkeys hopped down from the trees. Each monkey took a string of pearls.

One monkey did not hop down from the tree. That monkey had the queen's real pearls. It sat near the hole where it had put them.

The other monkeys danced around. They were very happy.

They told the monkey in the tree, "It is too bad you did not get a string of pearls. Look at *our* pearls. How beautiful they are! Look at our pearls! Look at our pearls!"

They kept saying this. "Look at our pearls! Look at our pearls!"

The monkey could not stand it any longer. The monkey reached into the hole. It pulled out the string of pearls.

"See *my* string of pearls!" it said. *"Your* pearls are made of glass. *My* pearls are real! I took them from the queen!"

Guards were hiding in the garden. They quickly caught the monkey. They took the monkey to the queen.

"Here are your pearls," they told the queen. "This monkey took your string of pearls."

The queen smiled. She said, "I knew that no one could get into my garden. And no one could get out. I wondered if a monkey took them."

The queen warned the monkey. Then she let the monkey go.

The queen thanked the guards. She said, "I am glad you found my pearls. You did your job. You did it very well."

The next night the queen had a party for the guards. She had the party in the garden.

The monkeys looked down from the trees. They watched the people eat and drink. The people all were very happy.

The monkeys were **delighted** too. For each one had a string of pearls. So what if their pearls were made of glass? They did not care.

Just one monkey was not happy. That monkey had no pearls at all. And you know who *that* monkey was.

TELL ABOUT THE STORY.

Put an X in the box next to the right answer. Each answer tells something (a *fact*) about the story.

1. The queen told a guard to
   - ☐ a. bring her some food.
   - ☐ b. take her to the lake.
   - ☐ c. watch her pearls.

2. The monkey took the pearls when the guard
   - ☐ a. fell asleep.
   - ☐ b. turned around.
   - ☐ c. went for a walk.

3. The monkey put the pearls
   - ☐ a. near some flowers.
   - ☐ b. under the chair.
   - ☐ c. in a hole in the tree.

4. The guards made pearls out of
   - ☐ a. stones.
   - ☐ b. glass.
   - ☐ c. wood.

END EACH LINE.

Finish the lines below. Fill in each empty space with one of the words in the box. Each word can be found in the story. There are five words and four empty spaces. This means that one word in the box will not be used.

Wild flowers can grow just about

_____. You can find them in
1

fields, in woods, and near

_____. Have you ever seen
2

flowers growing by the side of a

_____? Almost always, they
3

will be wild _____.
4

road	lakes
everywhere	
eyes	flowers

NUMBER CORRECT ☐ X 5 = ☐ YOUR SCORE

NUMBER CORRECT ☐ X 5 = ☐ YOUR SCORE

91

SHOW WHAT WORDS MEAN.

The words below are printed in **dark letters** in the story. You may look back at these vocabulary words before you answer the questions. Put an X in the box next to the right answer.

1. The queen prepared to swim. The word *prepared* means
    - ☐ a. got ready.
    - ☐ b. stayed home.
    - ☐ c. forgot about.

2. It put the pearls in a safe place. When something is *safe,*
    - ☐ a. it is big.
    - ☐ b. it can break.
    - ☐ c. nothing bad can happen to it.

3. She thought, "Perhaps a monkey took the pearls." The word *perhaps* means
    - ☐ a. it may be.
    - ☐ b. it cannot be.
    - ☐ c. it will be.

4. They were delighted with the pearls. The word *delighted* means
    - ☐ a. very angry.
    - ☐ b. very happy.
    - ☐ c. very worried.

THINK ABOUT THE STORY.

Here is how to answer these questions. First think about what happened in the story. Then work out the right answers. This is called *critical thinking.*

1. Which one is true?
    - ☐ a. A man got away with the pearls.
    - ☐ b. The guards did not look for the pearls.
    - ☐ c. The queen tricked the monkey.

2. The monkey took out the queen's pearls because the other monkeys
    - ☐ a. wanted to see them.
    - ☐ b. had no pearls.
    - ☐ c. kept showing off their pearls.

3. The story shows that the queen was
    - ☐ a. clever or bright.
    - ☐ b. not too clever.
    - ☐ c. very old.

4. The queen had a party because
    - ☐ a. it was her birthday.
    - ☐ b. she was happy with the guards.
    - ☐ c. the king was coming home.

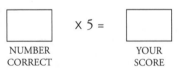

NUMBER CORRECT × 5 = YOUR SCORE

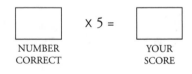

NUMBER CORRECT × 5 = YOUR SCORE

Spot Parts of a Story.

Stories have **characters**, a **plot**, and a **setting**. (See page 3.) Put an X in the box next to the right answer.

1. What happened first? (**Plot**)
   - ☐ a. The guard fell asleep.
   - ☐ b. The queen took off her pearls.
   - ☐ c. The monkey took the pearls.

2. What happened last? (**Plot**)
   - ☐ a. The queen had a party.
   - ☐ b. The queen went for a swim.
   - ☐ c. Guards caught the monkey.

3. Which best tells about the queen? (**Character**)
   - ☐ a. She did not like to take walks.
   - ☐ b. She never sat by the lake.
   - ☐ c. She thought a monkey might have taken the pearls.

4. Where does the story take place? (**Setting**)
   - ☐ a. in a house
   - ☐ b. in a garden
   - ☐ c. in some woods

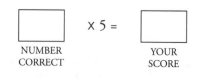

NUMBER CORRECT × 5 = YOUR SCORE

Think Some More About the Story.

Your teacher might want you to write your answers.

- Why did the queen think a monkey took the pearls?
- Why did the queen tell the guards to put glass pearls in the garden?
- At the end of the story, why was one monkey unhappy?

Write your scores in the box below. Then write your scores on pages 122 and 123.

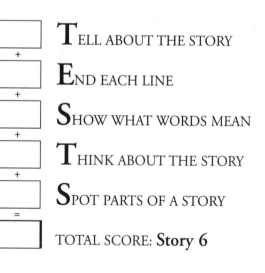

TELL ABOUT THE STORY

END EACH LINE

SHOW WHAT WORDS MEAN

THINK ABOUT THE STORY

SPOT PARTS OF A STORY

TOTAL SCORE: **Story 6**

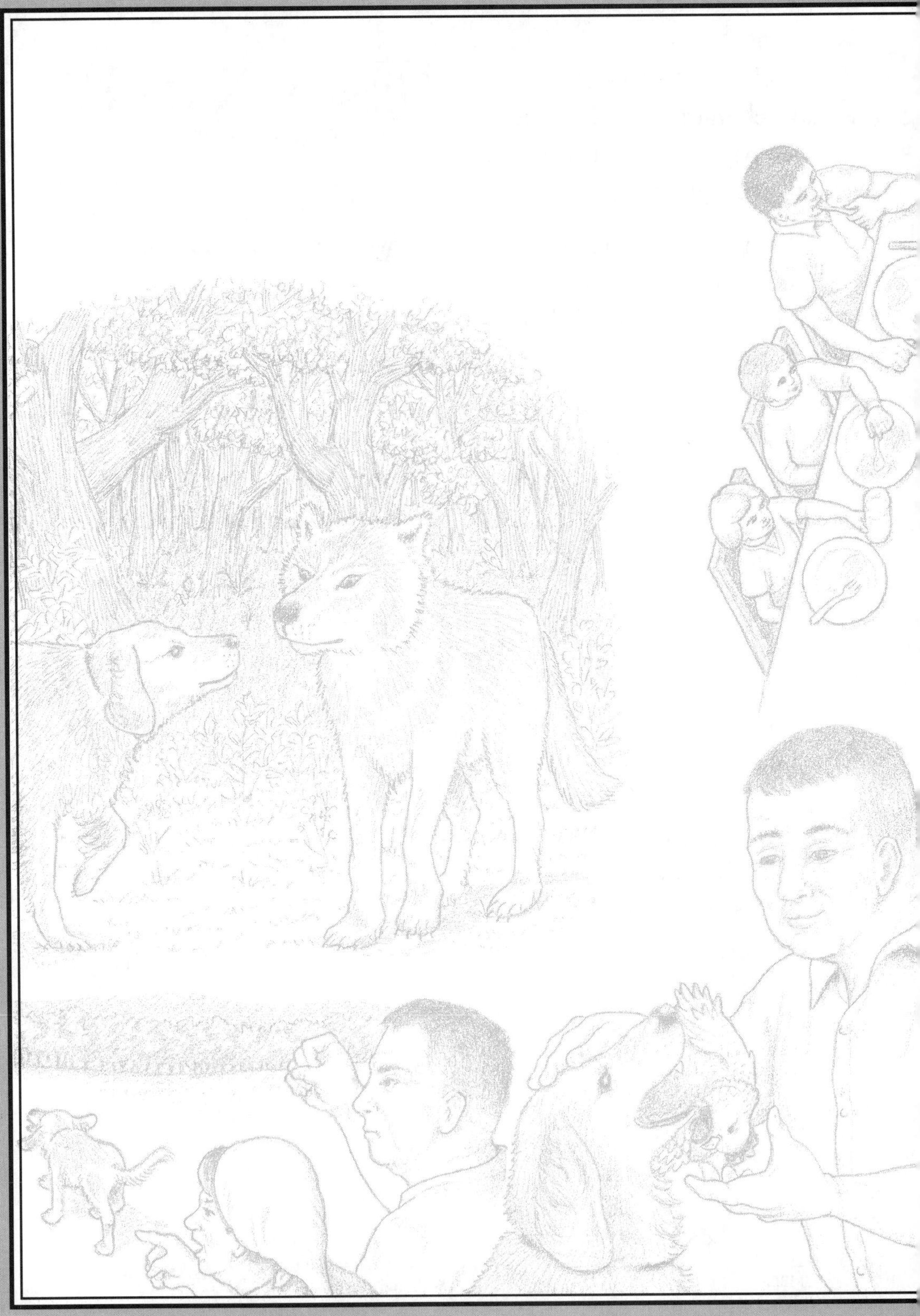

7
Work Well Done

a story from Russia

Before You Read

Before you read "Work Well Done," go over the words below. Make sure you know what each word means. This will help you when you read the story.

jobs: the work one does; different kinds of work. The dog did many *jobs* on the farm.

get rid of: do away with something. I want to *get rid of* my old clothes.

finally: at last; after some time. The dog *finally* caught up to the wolf.

arrived: came to a place. They *arrived* at the house on time.

Work Well Done

a story from Russia

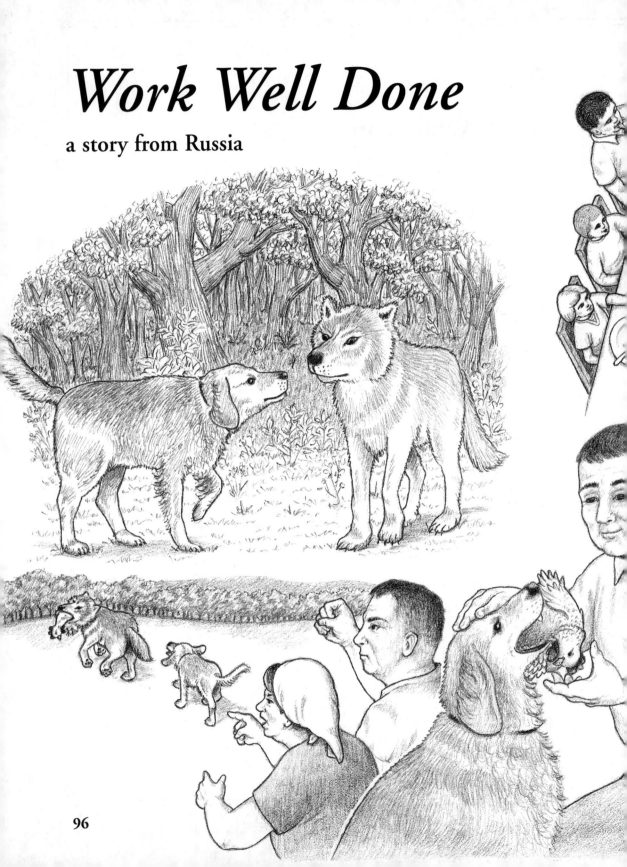

A farmer and his wife had a dog. It was a good dog. They had it for many years.

The dog was named Rex. The dog was a fine pet. But he also worked hard. He did many jobs on the farm.

He watched the house. When someone came near, he began to bark. The dog had a loud bark. It was easy to hear. When the dog barked, that meant someone was near.

There were some chickens on the farm. The farmer kept them behind the house. Rex had to watch over the chickens. Sometimes a wolf came out of the woods. The wolf wanted to eat the chickens. Then Rex ran at the wolf. He began to bark. He chased the wolf away.

The dog did these things for years. Then he got old. He could not bark very well. He could not run very fast. His legs were not strong.

One day the farmer and his wife were talking. The farmer said, "Rex has been a good dog. But now he is old. He cannot bark very well. He cannot run very fast. Still he must eat. We must pay for food."

"What do you think we should do?" asked the wife.

"Maybe we should get rid of him," the farmer said.

"You may be right," said the wife.

The farmer said, "I could take him far out into the woods. I could leave him there. He would not be able to find his way back. I might do that. I will think about it."

The dog heard them talking. He knew what they were saying. They did not want him any more. That made Rex sad.

Later that day Rex took a walk. He went into the woods. There he saw the wolf. The dog and the wolf knew each other. They were not friends. But they talked now and then.

"What is the matter?" asked the wolf. "You look very sad."

"Yes," Rex said. "I am very sad. The farmer and his wife say I am old. They do not want me anymore. They are going to leave me somewhere."

"What!" said the wolf. "They cannot do that! You have been a good dog. You watched the house well. You always kept me away from the chickens."

"I know," said Rex.

"Ah, well," said the wolf. "That is the way people are."

"There is nothing I can do," said Rex.

"I have an idea," said the wolf. "Go back to the farm. I will come by later. I will **grab** one of the chickens. I will take it and run. You can run after me. I will run to these woods. I will wait for you here. Then I will give you the chicken. You can take it back."

So that is what they did. The wolf came out of the woods. He found the biggest, fattest chicken. He took it and ran.

Rex began to bark. Then he ran after the wolf. The farmer and his wife saw it all.

The wolf ran into the woods. He waited for Rex. Rex finally caught up to him. The wolf gave the chicken to Rex. Rex brought it back to the farmer.

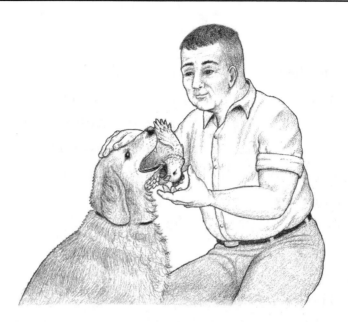

The farmer and his wife were happy. They said, "Rex is still a good dog. We will keep him a little longer."

The next night Rex went into the woods. He saw the wolf.

"Well, Rex," said the wolf. "How did everything go?"

Rex said, "Everything went very well. The farmer and his wife are happy with me now. They will keep me for a while."

"Ah," said the wolf. "That is good for you. But what about me? I did something for you. What will *you* do for *me?*"

Rex said, "I will do something for you. I heard the farmer and his wife. They are making a big dinner. It will be on Saturday night. Their son and his wife will come. They will bring their three children. There will be **plenty** of food."

"Food!" said the wolf. "Good! I love food!"

"Here is what to do," said the dog. "Come at six o'clock. Go to the back door. Wait there for me. Everyone will sit down to eat. Then I will push the door open. Come in. Go to the kitchen. It is by the back door. Take all the food you want. Then hurry away."

"Yes," said the wolf. "That is what I will do."

Saturday night came. The farmer's wife made a lot of good food. The son arrived with his wife. They brought their three children. One was a little boy. He was just two years old.

The family talked for a while. Then the farmer said, "Now let us eat."

They went to the dining room. They sat down at the table. It was piled high with food.

"Eat all you want," the farmer's wife said. "There is more in the kitchen."

Rex was watching them. He saw they were eating.

He went to the back door. He pushed the door open. There was the wolf.

"Come in," said Rex. "Go to the kitchen. Take the food that you want. Then hurry away. I must go back to the others."

The wolf went into the kitchen. There were many kinds of food. The wolf liked them all. What should he take? The wolf did not know. He ate a little of this. He ate a little of that. Everything was so good! He just kept on eating.

Rex sat near the table. He listened to the family talk.

The farmer said to his son, "Rex is old. Soon he will be too old to work. What should I do with him then?"

Just then the little boy climbed out of his chair. He went into the kitchen. But the wolf was still there! He was eating the food. He was eating and eating.

The little boy saw the wolf. The boy started to **scream.**

The family heard the child's cries. They **rushed** into the kitchen.

The farmer called out, "There is a wolf in the kitchen!"

The farmer's wife said, "He ran away with our chicken!"

The boy's mother cried out, "Now he will take away my baby!"

Rex came into the room. Rex saw the little boy. Rex saw the wolf. He began to bark at the wolf. The wolf turned around. It ran to the back door. Rex kept on barking. The wolf ran out the door. He ran back to the woods.

"Good dog!" said the farmer's son. "Good dog! Good Rex!"

He patted Rex on the head. Then the farmer's son said, "From now on, Rex will be our pet. He does not have to work. He can sit around all day. He can eat all he wants."

So Rex became that family's pet. He did not have to work. He sat around or played. And he had a lot of food to eat.

What happened to the wolf? Nobody knows. Rex never saw him again.

TELL ABOUT THE STORY.

Put an X in the box next to the right answer. Each answer tells something (a *fact*) about the story.

1. When someone came near the house, Rex would
   - ☐ a. bark.
   - ☐ b. cry.
   - ☐ c. run away.

2. The farmer said he might leave Rex
   - ☐ a. at home.
   - ☐ b. with a neighbor.
   - ☐ c. in the woods.

3. Rex told the wolf to
   - ☐ a. come in the front door.
   - ☐ b. wait at the back door.
   - ☐ c. eat all of the food.

4. The farmer's son said that Rex could
   - ☐ a. work for him.
   - ☐ b. stay in the yard.
   - ☐ c. be the family's pet.

END EACH LINE.

Finish the lines below. Fill in each empty space with one of the words in the box. Each word can be found in the story. There are five words and four empty spaces. This means that one word in the box will not be used.

Some wolves look very much like _____. But wolves have bigger feet and longer _____. The _____ is stronger than the dog. And wolves have short ears that always stand up _____.

legs		straight
	dogs	
night		wolf

SHOW WHAT WORDS MEAN.

The words below are printed in **dark letters** in the story. You may look back at these vocabulary words before you answer the questions. Put an X in the box next to the right answer.

1. The wolf said he would grab a chicken. The word *grab* means
    ☐ a. drop.
    ☐ b. take.
    ☐ c. help.

2. The farmer's wife made plenty of food. The word *plenty* means
    ☐ a. a lot of.
    ☐ b. very little.
    ☐ c. some.

3. The boy started to scream when he saw the wolf. When you *scream,* you
    ☐ a. call or cry out.
    ☐ b. do not move.
    ☐ c. jump up and down.

4. They all rushed into the kitchen. The word *rushed* means
    ☐ a. stopped.
    ☐ b. looked.
    ☐ c. hurried.

THINK ABOUT THE STORY.

Here is how to answer these questions. First think about what happened in the story. Then work out the right answers. This is called *critical thinking.*

1. Which one is true?
    ☐ a. Rex got lost in the woods.
    ☐ b. The wolf helped Rex.
    ☐ c. The child laughed at the wolf.

2. The wolf stayed in the kitchen a long time because it
    ☐ a. did not know how to get out.
    ☐ b. was waiting for the family.
    ☐ c. kept eating the food.

3. The farmer's son was very good to Rex because Rex
    ☐ a. chased the wolf away from the baby.
    ☐ b. could still work hard.
    ☐ c. liked to play with children.

4. At the end of the story, Rex must have felt
    ☐ a. happy.
    ☐ b. sad.
    ☐ c. worried.

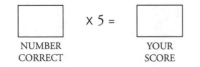

x 5 =

NUMBER CORRECT   YOUR SCORE

x 5 =

NUMBER CORRECT   YOUR SCORE

SPOT PARTS OF A STORY.

Stories have **characters**, a **plot**, and a **setting**. (See page 3.) Put an X in the box next to the right answer.

1. What happened first? (**Plot**)
   - ☐ a. The farmer thought about getting rid of Rex.
   - ☐ b. Rex let the wolf in the house.
   - ☐ c. The wolf ran away with a chicken.

2. What happened last? (**Plot**)
   - ☐ a. The farmer's son patted Rex.
   - ☐ b. Rex met the wolf in the woods.
   - ☐ c. The family sat down to eat.

3. Which best tells about Rex? (**Character**)
   - ☐ a. He was very lazy.
   - ☐ b. He worked hard for many years.
   - ☐ c. He was never sad.

4. Where does the story take place? (**Setting**)
   - ☐ a. in a big city
   - ☐ b. in a park
   - ☐ c. on a farm

☐ X 5 = ☐

NUMBER CORRECT   YOUR SCORE

THINK SOME MORE ABOUT THE STORY.

Your teacher might want you to write your answers.

- If you were the farmer, would you have wanted to get rid of Rex? Why?
- What if Rex had not chased the wolf out of the house? How do you think the story would have ended?
- At the end of the story, did you feel sorry for the wolf? Why?

Write your scores in the box below. Then write your scores on pages 122 and 123.

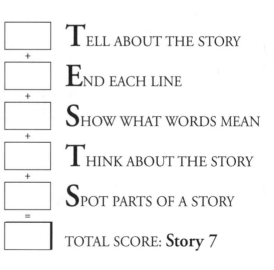

☐ **T**ELL ABOUT THE STORY
    +
☐ **E**ND EACH LINE
    +
☐ **S**HOW WHAT WORDS MEAN
    +
☐ **T**HINK ABOUT THE STORY
    +
☐ **S**POT PARTS OF A STORY
    =
☐ TOTAL SCORE: **Story 7**

8

The Snow Woman

an old story from Japan

Before You Read

Before you read "The Snow Woman," go over the words
below. Make sure you know what each word means. This
will help you when you read the story.

forest: land that is covered with trees. He cut down a tree
in the *forest*.

breath: the air that comes out of your mouth. On a cold
day, you can see your *breath*.

smoke: something that comes from a fire when it is
burning. Dark *smoke* came from the fire.

touch: to feel. Do not *touch* the animals in the zoo.

The Snow Woman

an old story from Japan

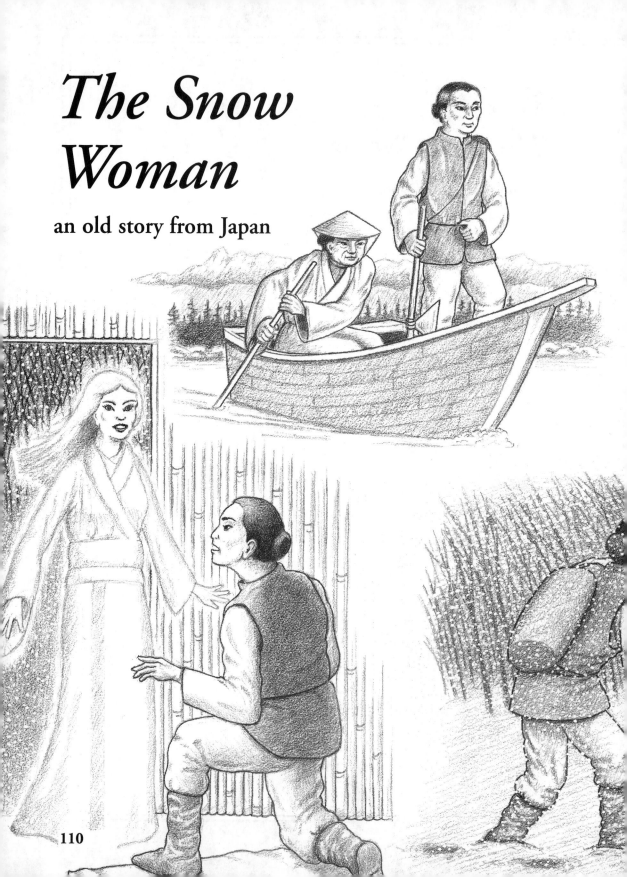

This story is strange. It is also very old. It was told more than 100 years ago.

This is the story of Niki. Niki was a woodcutter. He was 18 years old. He lived in a village in Japan.

One morning Niki went off to cut wood. He had to go to a forest. It was far from the village.

Niki walked for a long time. Then he came to a river. There was a man at the river. The man had a boat. The man took Niki across the river.

Niki worked all day. Evening came. Then Niki started for home. It had been snowing since noon. Now it was snowing very hard.

Niki thought, "What shall I do? I cannot swim across the river. I must find someplace to stay."

Niki looked around. He saw a very small house. It was made of wood. It was really just a **hut.** But it was better than nothing at all.

Niki hurried to the hut. He pushed open the door. No one was there.

Niki went inside. He pulled the door shut. The hut was so small, he could not make a fire. There was not even a window.

Niki lay down to rest. He thought, "It will stop snowing soon. The man with the boat will come back. Then he will take me across the river."

Niki could not sleep. He listened to the wind. It was very loud. He could also hear the snow. It kept hitting the hut.

Then Niki began to get cold. He got colder and colder. He had never felt so cold! Soon he fell asleep.

Suddenly Niki woke up. He felt snow against his face. The door of the hut was open. Snow was blowing in.

Niki saw a woman. She was walking through the snow. She was coming toward the hut.

Niki was surprised. He looked at the woman. She was a woman in white! She was as white as the snow. She seemed to be made out of snow. She was like a snow woman.

Now she was standing next to him. She was tall. Breath came out of her mouth. The breath looked like white smoke. Niki did not like the white smoke. He did not want it to touch him.

He thought, "The smoke must not touch me. If it does, I will die."

Niki saw that the woman was beautiful. But he was afraid of her.

She did not say a word. She kept looking at him. Then she said, "You are young. You are very young. I feel sorry for you."

She said softly, "I will not hurt you now. I will let you live. I will not let you die."

She went on, "But you must never talk about this. You must never say a word. Do not even tell your mother."

The woman turned to go. She said, "Remember! If you tell anyone about me, I will know. I will come back. And then you will die!"

The woman moved away from Niki. She went out the door.

At first Niki could not move. His legs were like stone. But soon he was able to walk. He went to the door. He looked out.

Where was the woman in white? Niki did not see her.

The snow was blowing hard. Niki closed the door. He put his back against it. Had it all been a **dream?** Had he really seen a woman in white? Or had he been looking at snow? Niki did not know.

Suddenly it stopped snowing. The sun began to **shine.** Niki went outside. He waited near the river. The man with the boat came back. The man took Niki across the river. Then Niki went home.

Niki felt **ill.** He got into bed. He stayed there for two days. Then he felt better. He started working again. He got up every morning. He went to the forest to cut wood. He did not say a word about the woman in white.

A year went by. One evening, Niki was going home. He saw a young woman. She was walking along the road.

"Good evening," Niki said.

"Good evening," she answered.

The woman was tall. Niki thought she was pretty. He walked next to her.

They began to talk. Her voice was very sweet. It was like the song of a bird. Niki liked her at once. And she seemed to like him.

She said, "My name is Olan. My mother and father are dead. I am going to Yedo. My grandmother lives there. I will live with her. She will help me find work."

Niki said, "You must be tired. You have walked for a long time. Come to my house. You can rest there for a while. My mother will make supper for you."

Olan thought about that. Then she said, "All right."

Niki's mother made supper for Olan. The two women got along very well. Niki's mother liked Olan very much. She said to Olan, "Stay here for a while. You can have your own room. You can work around the house. You can go to Yedo later. It is far away from here."

Olan said she would stay. She never did go to Yedo. She and Niki fell in love. A little later they got married.

Ten years went by. Niki and Olan were very happy. They had four children. They had two girls and two boys.

Everyone liked Olan very much. A neighbor said, "Olan is very good. She is a good mother. She is a good wife. She is very kind to Niki's mother. But Olan is not like us. All of us get older. But Olan does not. Olan stays the same. She looks as young as she was the day she came here."

One night the children were asleep. Olan was sitting in a chair. She was reading.

Niki sat next to her. He suddenly said, "Olan. I have been looking at you. Your face is so beautiful. It makes me think of something. It happened a long time ago. I was only 18 years old. I saw someone then. She was as beautiful as you."

Niki stopped talking. He was looking at Olan. "Yes," he said. "She was also tall. She was very much like you."

Olan did not say a word.

Niki went on. He told her about the time in the hut. He told her about the woman in white. He called her "the snow woman."

He said, "She was the only woman I ever saw who was as beautiful as you. But she was only a dream. I mean . . . I *think* she was a dream. I have never been sure."

Suddenly Olan threw down what she was reading. She stood up. She was very angry. She said, "That was no dream! It was I! I was the woman in the snow! I told you never to say a word about that! Remember? I said you would die if you did!"

Niki looked at Olan. She was angry. But she also looked sad.

Olan said, "I should not let you live. I gave my word."

She kept looking at Niki. She said softly, "But I love you very much. And I love our children. What should I do?"

Then she said, "There is only one thing to do. I must leave you now. I must leave our home. I must leave our children."

Niki was very surprised. He could not talk. He could not say a word.

Olan moved to the door. Then she went outside. Niki found his voice. "Wait, Olan!" he cried. Niki hurried to the door. He looked around. But Olan was gone. He never saw her again.

TELL ABOUT THE STORY.

Put an X in the box next to the right answer. Each answer tells something (a *fact*) about the story.

1. Niki went to the forest to
   - ☐ a. hunt animals.
   - ☐ b. cut wood.
   - ☐ c. look for a lost friend.

2. The woman in white seemed to be made out of
   - ☐ a. stone.
   - ☐ b. glass.
   - ☐ c. snow.

3. The woman in white said that Niki should
   - ☐ a. tell his mother what happened.
   - ☐ b. never say a word about what happened.
   - ☐ c. go home at once.

4. Olan told Niki that she
   - ☐ a. was the woman in the snow.
   - ☐ b. would never leave him.
   - ☐ c. did not love their children.

END EACH LINE.

Finish the lines below. Fill in each empty space with one of the words in the box. Each word can be found in the story. There are five words and four empty spaces. This means that one word in the box will not be used.

There are places where it snows all the _____. But there
₁
are also places where it never snows at _____. Are you used to
₂
seeing snow fall from the _____? Or are you one of the
₃
many people who have never seen _____?
₄

sky		colder
	time	
all		snow

 X 5 = ☐

NUMBER CORRECT   YOUR SCORE

119

SHOW WHAT WORDS MEAN.

The words below are printed in **dark letters** in the story. You may look back at these vocabulary words before you answer the questions. Put an X in the box next to the right answer.

1. Niki pushed open the door of the hut. What is a *hut?*
   - ☐ a. a big building
   - ☐ b. a small house
   - ☐ c. a little boat

2. Did it happen, or was it a dream? A *dream* is
   - ☐ a. a long night.
   - ☐ b. a lot of snow.
   - ☐ c. what you see when you are sleeping.

3. The sun began to shine. The word *shine* means to
   - ☐ a. be bright with light.
   - ☐ b. get very dark.
   - ☐ c. fall slowly.

4. Niki was ill and stayed at home. When you are *ill,* you
   - ☐ a. work hard.
   - ☐ b. feel well.
   - ☐ c. do not feel well.

THINK ABOUT THE STORY.

Here is how to answer these questions. First think about what happened in the story. Then work out the right answers. This is called *critical thinking.*

1. The snow woman did not kill Niki because
   - ☐ a. he ran away from her.
   - ☐ b. it was too cold.
   - ☐ c. she felt sorry for him.

2. Which one is true?
   - ☐ a. Olan was very short.
   - ☐ b. Olan did not seem to get older.
   - ☐ c. Olan lived with her grandmother.

3. Olan was angry at Niki because he
   - ☐ a. told her about the snow woman.
   - ☐ b. was not a good father.
   - ☐ c. did not love her.

4. If Niki had not told Olan about the snow woman, Olan would have
   - ☐ a. gone away.
   - ☐ b. made him tell her the story.
   - ☐ c. stayed with him.

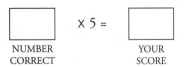

X 5 =

NUMBER CORRECT   YOUR SCORE

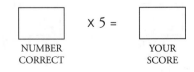

X 5 =

NUMBER CORRECT   YOUR SCORE

Spot parts of a story.

Stories have **characters,** a **plot,** and a **setting.** (See page 3.) Put an X in the box next to the right answer.

1. What happened last? (**Plot**)
   - ☐ a. Niki's mother made supper for Olan.
   - ☐ b. Niki saw the woman.
   - ☐ c. Olan said, "I must leave our home."

2. Which best tells about Olan? (**Character**)
   - ☐ a. She did not get along with Niki's mother.
   - ☐ b. She was beautiful and different from other people.
   - ☐ c. The neighbors did not like her.

3. Where does the story take place? (**Setting**)
   - ☐ a. in Japan
   - ☐ b. in England
   - ☐ c. in the United States

4. When does the story take place? (**Setting**)
   - ☐ a. a year ago
   - ☐ b. 10 years ago
   - ☐ c. many years ago

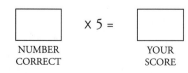

NUMBER CORRECT   X 5 =   YOUR SCORE

Think some more about the story.

Your teacher might want you to write your answers.
- Why do you think the snow woman let Niki live?
- A neighbor said that Olan was "not like us." How was she different?
- Why did Olan go away at the end of the story?

Write your scores in the box below. Then write your scores on pages 122 and 123.

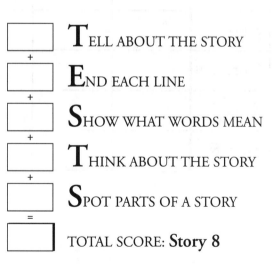

☐   **T**ELL ABOUT THE STORY
+
☐   **E**ND EACH LINE
+
☐   **S**HOW WHAT WORDS MEAN
+
☐   **T**HINK ABOUT THE STORY
+
☐   **S**POT PARTS OF A STORY
=
☐   TOTAL SCORE: **Story 8**

121

Progress Chart

1. Write in your score for each exercise.
2. Write in your TOTAL SCORE.

	T	E	S	T	S	TOTAL SCORE
Story 1						
Story 2						
Story 3						
Story 4						
Story 5						
Story 6						
Story 7						
Story 8						

Progress Graph

1. Write your TOTAL SCORE in the box under the number for each story.
2. Put an X along the line above each box to show your TOTAL SCORE for that story.
3. Draw a line from X to X to see how much your scores go up.

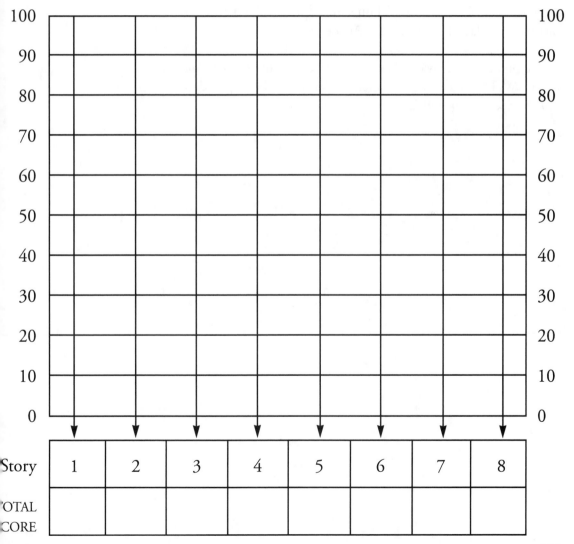

Story	1	2	3	4	5	6	7	8
TOTAL SCORE								

Acknowledgments

Acknowledgment is gratefully made to the following publishers, authors, and agents for permission to reprint these works. Every effort has been made to determine copyright owners. In the case of any omissions, the Publisher will be pleased to make suitable acknowledgments in future editions.

"Across Time" from *Across the Seas of Time* by Lael J. Littke. Copyright © 1977. Previously published in STORY WORLD. Copyright © 1977 by D. C. Thomson. Reprinted by permission of Larry Sternig/Jack Byrne Literary Agency.

"Morning Sunshine" was suggested by a passage in *West African Folktales* by W. H. Barker and C. Sinclair. George G. Harrap and Company, London, 1917.